shown was 75 miles distant."
"Up and Atom" City
Vegas, Nevada
HERE IT IS!
The famous
CLU
ICONS
LIQUOR
STORES
HOTEL
FREE
D0596728

# LAS VEGAS

## VINTAGE GRAPHICS FROM SIN CITY

EDITED BY JIM HEIMANN / INTRODUCTION BY W. R. WILKERSON III

**TASCHEN**

KÖLN LONDON LOS ANGELES MADRID PARIS TOKYO

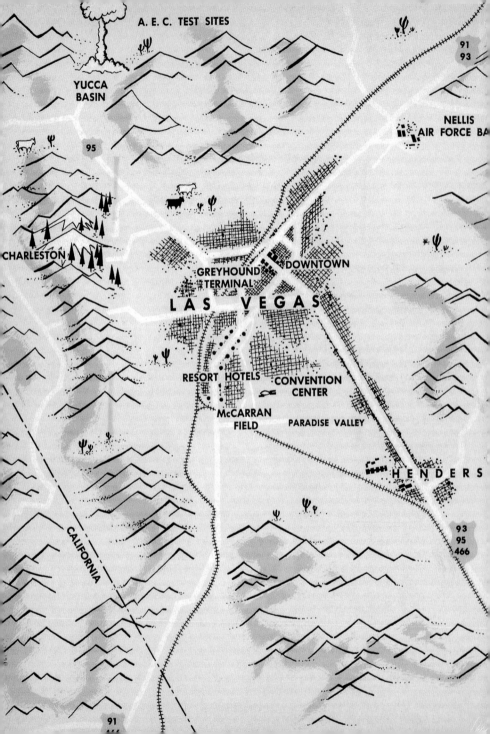

BNA 2005     3/3/05

F 849 .L35 L37 2003

## THE STRIP (1970s)

1. HACIENDA HOTEL
2. DUNES HOTEL
3. CAESARS PALACE
4. THE CASTAWAYS
5. FRONTIER HOTEL
6. SILVER SLIPPER
7. STARDUST HOTEL
8. CIRCUS CIRCUS
9. TROPICANA HOTEL
10. ALADDIN HOTEL
11. BONANZA HOTEL
12. FLAMINGO HOTEL
13. SANDS HOTEL
14. DESERT INN HOTEL
15. RIVIERA HOTEL
16. LANDMARK HOTEL
17. THUNDERBIRD HOTEL
18. SAHARA HOTEL
19. INTERNATIONAL HOTEL*
20. CONVENTION CENTER
21. SHOWBOAT HOTEL
22. SILVER NUGGET

*BECAME LAS VEGAS HILTON, JUNE 1971.

## DOWNTOWN LAS VEGAS (1950s)

GREYHOUND BUS TERMINAL   DEPOT

**MAIN STREET**

GOLDEN GATE
MONTE CARLO    LAS VEGAS CLUB
THE WESTERNER
NEW PIONEER CLUB    SILVER PALACE

1ST STREET

CALIFORNIA CLUB    BIRD CAGE
NEVADA CLUB    THE MINT
LUCKY STRIKE CLUB    BOULDER CLUB
GOLDEN NUGGET    HORSESHOE CLUB

2ND STREET

FREMONT HOTEL

NELLIS AIR FORCE BASE

TO DEATH VALLEY

TO LAKE MEAD

N. MAIN STREET

95

91 93

22

15

*Las Vegas*

21

FREMONT STREET

LAS VEGAS BOULEVARD

# VIVA LAS VEGAS

IT BEGAN AS A DUSTY FRONTIER TOWN OF SMALL CASINOS, WITH A CAST LIKE THAT OF AN OLD WESTERN MOVIE, AND EVOLVED INTO SIN CITY: A UNIVERSE OF NEON WELDED AROUND GAMBLING AND PROSTITUTION, LUBRICATED BY THE MACHINERY OF ORGANIZED CRIME AND THE MASS-PRODUCTION OF WORLD-CLASS ENTERTAINMENT. IT WAS THE FIRST CITY TO BECOME AN AMERICAN THEME-PARK ICON. THE WORLD KNOWS IT AS LAS VEGAS.

## THE NEW FRONTIER (1829-1930)

A young scout named Rafael Rivera first set foot in the area in 1829. He called the springs he discovered there Las Vegas, derived from the Spanish word for "the mead-ows", although the name hardly applied. Rather, the locale could claim to be one of the hottest spots in North America, a place where the excruciating heat during the sum-mer months soared passed the century mark and the temperatures in winter could eas-ily dip into freezing. The Mojave desert was simply a place to endure, a wasteland trav-elers passed through on their way to the coast.

In 1844, civilian pathfinder John C. Fremont led a U. S. Army expedition to Las Vegas to map the territory. They did not stay long. A decade later, thirty devout, Mormon mis-sionaries from nearby Utah established a fort there to protect a Congressionally man-dated mail route from Salt Lake City to San Diego. But years of harsh conditions, inter-nal bickering and a brutal Indian raid in 1857 sent them home to Salt Lake.

In the end, it took the railroad to create Las Vegas, to transform the site from nowhere into somewhere. In 1862, Congress passed a charter authorizing the Union Pacific Railroad to connect to the Central Pacific Railroad's tracks at the California border. Las Vegas, Nevada (the latter was granted statehood in 1864) had its official founding on May 15, 1905 as the last railroad spike was pounded into the desert floor. Travelers on their way to the California coastline could now cross the unrelenting desert in a fraction of the time it took by covered wagon or horseback.

It did not take long for the seeds of entrepreneurship to germinate. The first major hotel, a thirty-room, canvas-topped affair called Hotel Las Vegas, soon opened for busi-ness. Two years later, in 1907, downtown's Fremont Street turned on its first electric street lights, powered by a ninety-horsepower, single-cylinder engine called Old Betsy. An economy straight out of the Wild West dominated: ranching, cattle and horses remained staples through the 1930s and, even though artesian wells were discovered which could have supported it, the valley would never become an agricultural region.

Gambling, prostitution and booze had been legal since statehood. In 1906, however, they were restricted to a rowdy area on the north side of town known as Block 16, the city's red-light district,and home to Las Vegas' first luxury establishment, the Arizona Club.

In 1910, the city suffered a major setback. Under pressure from the local Women's Civic and Anti-Gambling Leagues, state legislators passed a measure prohibiting all forms of gambling. Although illegal, the practice was still tolerated, provided it was relegated to the back rooms of bars and clubs. Realizing that the city's future did not belong to the railroad but to the car, Las Vegas spent $10 000 creating the road to Jean (near the state line), which was the beginning of Route 91. By 1925, all the streets in downtown Las Vegas were paved, and less than twenty years later hotels would be constructing vast parking lots at their front entrances to welcome motorists.

## THE SAWDUST ERA (1931-1940)

Hardly a tourist destination by this time in its history, Nevada's flagging economy desperately needed a boost, and 1931 was the year it received the three gifts that really put Vegas on the map. First, the Boulder Canyon Project Act, which U.S. President Calvin Coolidge had signed in 1928, spurred the construction of the world's largest arch-gravity dam, at a cost of nearly $49 million. The purpose of Hoover Dam, some thirty miles from Las Vegas, was to bring power to the West and relief from the Depression. It became the largest public works project in American history and resulted in an influx of thousands of workers. The second gift came in March: Governor Fred Balzar signed a "wide-open gambling bill" that made Nevada the first state in the union to embrace legalized gambling. Finally, statewide divorce law became the most lenient in the nation when the state legislature lowered residency requirements from three months to six weeks.

Las Vegas boomed. Two-story brick structures replaced one-story wood shacks and the city's trophy was the three-story, hundred-room Apache hotel built in 1932. Casinos flourished along Fremont Street, an area known as Glitter Gulch. Locals referred to the casinos as "sawdust joints" because of the sawdust on their floors. With new sidewalks and storefronts, Las Vegas was looking more and more like Main Street, U.S.A., but with legalized gambling as its main economy.

History credits Tom Hull with the vision of housing a nightclub, casino and hotel under one roof in his 1941 establishment, El Rancho Vegas. This concept, however, was in fact the brainchild of a notable underworld figure from Los Angeles, Tony Cornero, who opened the Meadows Club on May 2, 1931 along the Boulder Highway. History would also have us believe that organized crime arrived in Las Vegas with noted Los Angeles gangster Benjamin "Bugsy" Siegel in 1946; but Cornero was likewise responsible for importing its insidious influence to Southern Nevada, a move that heralded the beginnings of organized crime's grip over the city.

In 1934, the city gained another gift: neon, which announced its arrival from Paris with the marquee outside the Boulder Club. The colorful signs floating against the dark, desert sky multiplied and drew visitors year after year like moths to a porch light. The neon surge in the mid-forties included the Pioneer Club's neon cowboy on Fremont Street and the signs outside the Las Vegas and Monte Carlo Clubs. A quantum leap came in 1958 when the Stardust lit up the night with its neon galaxy of comets and planets, 216 feet long and 27 feet high.

If the lights drew onlookers, it was gambling that drew the spenders. Until police reform enforcing Los Angeles' ban on gambling and prostitution came into effect in 1938, Hollywood had all the elements of Las Vegas before there was a Las Vegas. Thriving casinos such as the Clover and Colony Clubs dotted the Sunset Strip; bordellos hid in plain sight just off the drag; and nightclubs and restaurants offered exquisite fine dining and the top entertainment in the country. The Sunset Strip was a glamorous world where movie stars and Hollywood's elite congregated. All that changed, however, in the midst of a municipal scandal, when reform candidate Fletcher Bowron won the '38 mayor's race and shut down gambling and prostitution in L.A. Only racetracks such as Santa Anita were not effected. The house-cleaning forced L.A. gamblers to brave the six-hour road trip (without the benefit of air-conditioning) to the only state in the union with legalized gambling. The highway lacked the convenience stores and gas stations that now populate the drive and many travelers stashed extra cans of gas in the trunks of their cars. Had it not been for the '38 gambling shutdown in California, Las Vegas as we know it would never have come to be.

## THE RESORT ERA (1941-1957)

The transformation of Las Vegas from modest desert oasis to tourist destination began at the start of World War II. Defense workers from the nearby airbase flocked to Vegas, eager to spend their money. The Army threatened to make the town off-limits to military personnel if it did not crack down on prostitution, and nearly a decade later the county finally banned the practice. (One could still visit Pahrump, NV, an hour away, to indulge in legally sanctioned sex-for-sale.) Gambling, however, remained strong, with revenues jumping 56 percent between 1941 and 1944. Not limiting itself to the title of divorce capital of America, Las Vegas also became its wedding capital. In 1942, over twenty thousand marriage licenses were issued by Clark County, with most weddings taking place in the city's little, roadside chapels.

The now-famous Las Vegas Strip began outside city limits in 1941 with Los Angeles hotel magnate Thomas Hull's El Rancho Vegas – designed as a luxurious dude ranch, but more motor hotel than resort by today's standards. Hull saw the potential for tourism and built his hotel right on Route 91, an unincorporated part of Clark County where taxes were significantly lower and building codes more lenient.

In 1946, Hollywood publisher and restaurateur (and father of this author) Billy Wilkerson took Hull's resort concept to the next level and named the hotel after his favorite bird, the flamingo. Wanting to give guests more than just a bed and some entertainment, he envisaged a two hundred-room playground for gamblers with first-rate entertainment, food and service wrapped in a European setting. He designed his thirty-three-acre, self-contained universe so that the visitor would have no thoughts of leaving, integral to which was his revolutionary installation of air-conditioning. Until now, most hotels had only electric ceiling fans or crude swamp coolers that churned the hot desert air, and Wilkerson's gamble on air-conditioning made the desert at long last inhabitable. It was also Wilkerson who named the Strip after that on Sunset Boulevard, where his successful nightclubs and restaurants – like Ciro's and La Rue's – lined the street. His prediction that the dusty highway on which he was building would one day be shoulder-to-shoulder with hotels eventually came true.

The nightclub impresario did, however, have a fatal flaw: he was a chronic gambler. He had completed only half of the Flamingo when he lost his construction funds on the tables. Wilkerson was partnered with Bugsy Siegel, who was used to calling the shots and demanded more control of the project, threatening to kill Wilkerson when he refused to relinquish the reins. It was not a matter of *if*, but *where* and *when*, so Wilkerson fled to Paris. Five months later, in June of 1947, the young, handsome gangster was shot dead in the home of his girlfriend, Virginia Hill, who was also hiding out in Paris.

With the 1948 opening of McCarran Field, the first airport in hundreds of miles, Las Vegas became an international tourist destination. The city saw an explosion of new hotels, most of them built on the Strip: the Desert Inn (1950); the Sahara and Sands (1952); the Royal Nevada, Dunes and the Strip's first high-rise, the Riviera (1955); and the Hacienda (1956). Downtown's fifteen-story Fremont (1956) stood as the tallest building in the state. Hotel construction costs skyrocketed from $5 million in the early fifties to $15 million with the building of the Tropicana in 1957. Room counts also increased, from three hundred at the beginning of the decade to the one thousand contained in the '58 Stardust. Hotels were beginning to develop and emphasize grandiose themes. The Dunes' Arabic motif, for example, set the tone for the baroque confections that later crowded the Strip. The mega-resort was here to stay.

## THE ENTERTAINMENT ERA (1958–1965)

The fifties also rendered Las Vegas synonymous with entertainment. Many celebrities, from Frank Sinatra to Judy Garland, first lit up the Las Vegas stage in this decade. The town hosted lavish floorshow productions such as the "Lido de Paris" and the "Folies Bergère". Ironically, the performer who would become largest draw of all time in Las Vegas entertainment history flopped initially. In 1956, Elvis Presley's raucous hip-swiveling review failed to appeal to the Frank Sinatra set.

The prosperous Las Vegas of the late fifties to early sixties was not without controversy. In the midst of a thriving entertainment scene, black performers were still denied use of hotel facilities, and in 1958 they refused to sign any contracts until such facilities were made available to them. Behind the glitz were the feuding gangsters, who dominated the entertainers performing in their hotels, not to mention the gambling fixes, drugs, illegal prostitution and boxing matches. Above-ground nuclear tests conducted at the Nevada Test Site northwest of Las Vegas were a continual thorn in the side of hotel operators, who declared that seeing mushroom clouds from their doorsteps was bad for business.

The decade ended on a positive note with the birth of superstar entertainment on the Strip, which happened quite by chance. On January 20, 1960, during the filming of the Warner Bros classic "Ocean's Eleven", Peter Lawford, Frank Sinatra, Dean Martin, Sammy Davis Jr. and Joey Bishop commandeered the stage at the Sands for a three-week, onstage party that lasted until the early hours of each morning. The press billed it as the "Summit Meeting at the Sands", but the performers were immortalized simply as the Rat Pack.

## THE THEME ERA (1966–1979)

By the mid-sixties, Las Vegas was again under new management. If Billy Wilkerson's Flamingo hotel was the midwife that ushered organized crime into the city on a large scale, business magnate and publicity recluse Howard Hughes was the camel driver who sent them packing. During his four-year tenure he snapped up the Frontier, Desert Inn, Sands, Silver Slipper, Landmark and Castaways, earning the title of Vegas' biggest landlord. It was during Hughes' reign that the concept of Las Vegas as a family destination was born, beginning with the opening of Caesars Palace in 1966 and Circus Circus in '68. Hotels continued to grow in size during the seventies. The MGM Grand, named after the film company that had invested in it, opened in 1972 with 2100 rooms.

Thirteen years after his unsuccessful cabaret debut, Elvis Presley made a triumphant return to Las Vegas, becoming the biggest earner in the city's history. The revenues of hotels and casinos on the Strip were said to jump an average of 10 percent when the king of rock and roll performed, and no other entertainer to date has challenged that legacy.

## THE CORPORATE ERA (1980–2000)

Mass-scale car production was born in 1917 in Dearborn, Michigan with the creation of Henry Ford's River Rouge factory. From the 1980s on, Las Vegas emulated the car manufacturer's template by creating a gargantuan production line single-mindedly devoted to recreation. Despite Hughes' earlier attempts, it was not until this period that Las Vegas was truly recognized as an icon of American popular culture. Hotels' guest room counts jumped from two to three thousand and their grounds housed everything from exotic animals to full-size, theme-park roller coasters. By the year 2000, over one hundred and twenty thousand couples were exchanging vows annually.

Many older properties scrambled to upgrade. In 1982, the old Thunderbird reopened as the new El Rancho after a $25-million facelift. Las Vegas had an explosive year in 1986, recording 14.2 million visitors in the first eleven months, which drove other hotels, like the Aladdin, to upgrade posthaste.

The corporate era was truly ushered in, however, by liquor distributor Steve Wynn, who cashed in on a well-timed real estate deal and sunk his profits into the mammoth, half-billion dollar Mirage. Occupying 86 acres on the Strip and filling 3,303 guest rooms, it remains the largest private hotel in the world. Wynn demonstrated that gamblers preferred an attractive setting to the noisy, congested spaces typical of other hotels. With the opening of the Mirage in 1989, the die was cast for the future of Las Vegas hotels. A period of frenetic construction ensued, resulting in the Excalibur (1990); the Luxor and Treasure Island, each exceeding the two thousand-room mark, and the MGM Grand hotel's theme park renovation (1993); the Stratosphere (1996), which boasted the tallest observation tower in the U.S.; New York-New York (1997); the Bellagio (1998); and the Venetian, Mandalay Bay and Paris Las Vegas (1999). Wynn struck a cord with the elegant Bellagio (Italian for "elegant relaxation") inspired by

Italy's Lake Como. The thirty-six-story resort, complete with an eight-and-a-half-acre lake, lured serious gamblers who felt lost in the melee of family entertainment.

All this development, however, came at a historical cost. Room had to be made for the riveting panorama of volcanoes and castles, European capitals and pirate adventures, and the Dunes, Sands and Hacienda were all demolished, making way for new structures to rise from their dust.

Las Vegas never developed methodically. The city is remarkable for the fact that it periodically sheds its skin and re-invents itself. Its evolution is a collage of mistakes, experiments, practical solutions and chaotic visions which, since 1931, has produced an inventory of one hundred and thirty thousand rooms sandwiched along a three-and-a-half-mile highway that was once just barren desert, $7.2 billion in annual gambling revenues and thirty-six million tourists a year – all woven around the something-for-nothing ethos of casino gambling and making it the capital of consumerism, capitalism and American kitsch.

# VIVA LAS VEGAS

WAS EINMAL EIN STAUBIGES WILDWESTKAFF GEWESEN WAR, MIT EIN PAAR KLEINEN KASINOS UND EINWOHNERN, WIE MAN SIE AUS EINEM AL-TEN WESTERN KENNT, ENTWICKELTE SICH ZUM AMERIKANISCHEN SÜN-DENBABEL, ZU „SIN CITY": EINE NEONWELT, DIE SICH UM GLÜCKSSPIEL UND PROSTITUTION DREHTE, ANGETRIEBEN VON DER MASCHINERIE DES ORGANISIERTEN VERBRECHENS UND DER UNTERHALTUNGSINDUSTRIE. SIE WAR DIE ERSTE STADT, DIE ZUM INBEGRIFF DES AMERIKANISCHEN ERLEBNISPARKS WURDE. IHR NAME: LAS VEGAS.

## DER WILDE WESTEN (1829-1930)

Ein junger Scout namens Rafael Rivera kam 1829 erstmals in die Gegend. Er nannte die Oase, die er dort entdeckte, „Las Vegas", spanisch für „Die Wiesen", auch wenn der Name kaum unpassender hätte sein können. Der Ort konnte vielmehr für sich bean-spruchen, einer der heißesten Flecken Nordamerikas zu sein, eine Gegend, in der die sengende Hitze in den Sommermonaten auf über 40 Grad stieg, während die Tempe-raturen im Winter unter den Gefrierpunkt fallen konnten. Die Mojavewüste war eine Einöde, die Reisende auf dem Weg zur Küste durchqueren und erdulden mussten.

1844 führte der Forscher und Pfadfinder John C. Fremont eine zivile Expedition der US Army nach Las Vegas, die das Gebiet vermessen sollte. Sie blieben nicht lang. Ein Jahrzehnt später errichteten 30 fromme Mormonenmissionare aus der nahe gelege-nen Region Utah ein Fort, um die vom Kongress angeordnete Postroute von Salt Lake City nach San Diego zu schützen. Doch nach Jahren unter harten Lebensbedingungen, nach internen Streitigkeiten und einem brutalen Indianerüberfall 1857 kehrten sie heim an den Großen Salzsee.

Erst die Eisenbahn sicherte Las Vegas einen Platz auf der Landkarte. 1862 beauf-tragte der Kongress die Union Pacific Railroad, die Verbindung mit den Gleisen der Central Pacific Railroad an der kalifornischen Grenze herzustellen. Der 15. Mai 1905, als der letzte Schienennagel in den Wüstenboden gerammt wurde, gilt als offizielles Gründungsdatum von Las Vegas, Nevada. Reisende an die kalifornische Küste konn-ten die erbarmungslose Wüste jetzt in einem Bruchteil der Zeit durchqueren, die man mit Pferd oder Planwagen dafür benötigt hatte.

Es dauerte nicht lange, bis sich der Unternehmergeist regte. Das erste richtige Hotel mit 30 Zimmern und einem Segeltuchdach öffnete unter dem Namen „Hotel Las Vegas" bald seine Pforten. 1907, zwei Jahre später, gingen im Ortskern auf der Fremont Street die ersten elektrischen Lichter an, die von einem Ein-Zylinder-Generator namens Old Betsy angetrieben wurden. Es herrschte eine echte Wildwest-Wirtschaft: Bis in die 30er Jahre hinein blieben Viehzucht und Pferde die Haupterwerbszweige.

Glücksspiel, Prostitution und Alkohol waren seit der Staatsgründung erlaubt. 1906 waren sie jedoch noch auf eine zwielichtige Gegend im Norden der Stadt begrenzt, die als Block 16 bekannt war – ein Rotlichtbezirk, in dem auch das erste Luxus-Etablissement lag, der Arizona Club.

1910 erlitt die Stadt einen schweren Rückschlag. Unter dem Druck des örtlichen Frauenvereins und der Liga zum Verbot des Glücksspiels erließ die Regierung des Staates Nevada ein Gesetz, das alle Arten von Glücksspiel verbot; es wurde damit illegal, war aber geduldet, solange es auf die Hinterzimmer von Kneipen und Clubs beschränkt blieb. Las Vegas begriff früh, dass seine Zukunft dem Automobil und nicht der Eisenbahn gehörte und wendete 10 000 Dollar für den Bau der Straße nach Jean auf, die den Anfang der Route 91 bildete. 1925 waren bereits alle Straßen in der Innenstadt asphaltiert und nicht einmal 20 Jahre später wurden riesige Parkplätze vor den Hotels gebaut, um die Autofahrer willkommen zu heißen.

## DIE SÄGEMEHL-ÄRA (1931–1940)

Von Tourismus konnte zu dieser Zeit noch keine Rede sein und Nevadas am Boden liegende Wirtschaft brauchte dringend Auftrieb. 1931 war das Jahr, in dem Las Vegas drei Geschenke bekam, die ihm seine spätere Bedeutung sicherten. Das erste war der 1928 unterzeichnete „Boulder Canyon Project Act", der den Bau der größten Bogengewichtsstaumauer der Welt antrieb. Zweck des etwa 50 km von Las Vegas entfernt gelegenen Hoover-Staudamms war es, dem Westen Strom zu bringen und die Große Depression zu bekämpfen. Er wurde das größte öffentliche Bauvorhaben der amerikanischen Geschichte und führte zum Zuzug von Tausenden von Arbeitern. Das zweite Geschenk kam im März: Gouverneur Fred Balzar unterzeichnete ein Gesetz, mit dem Nevada zum ersten amerikanischen Bundesstaat wurde, der das Glücksspiel gesetzlich erlaubte. Und schließlich wurde das Scheidungsrecht zum liberalsten im ganzen Land.

Las Vegas wurde zur Boomtown. Zweistöckige Backsteinhäuser ersetzten flache Holzhütten, der Stolz der Stadt war das dreigeschossige, im Jahre 1932 erbaute Apache Hotel mit 100 Zimmern. In der „Glitzerschlucht" an der Fremont Street, der „Glitter Gulch", florierten die Spielhöllen. Mit den neuen Bürgersteigen und Schaufensterauslagen wirkte Las Vegas allmählich immer mehr wie eine durchschnittliche amerikanische Kleinstadt – nur dass der Haupterwerbszweig hier das legale Glücksspiel war.

Tom Hull gilt als derjenige, der als Erster in seinem visionären Etablissement El Rancho Vegas Nachtclub, Spielkasino und Hotel unter einem Dach vereinigte. Das Konzept stammte jedoch in Wahrheit von einer berühmt-berüchtigten Unterweltgröße, Tony Cornero, der am 2. Mai 1931 den Meadows Club eröffnete. Den Legenden zufolge kam das organisierte Verbrechen mit dem bekannten Gangster Benjamin „Bugsy" Siegel 1946 von Los Angeles nach Las Vegas, doch tatsächlich war es Cornero, mit dessen Ankunft der unheilvolle Einfluss der Mafia in Nevada Einzug hielt, bis diese die Stadt schließlich fest in ihrem Griff hatte.

1934 wurde die Stadt wieder einmal beschenkt: mit Neon, das in Form einer großen Leuchtschrift für den Boulder Club aus Paris eintraf. Bald gab es immer mehr der bunten, vor dem dunklen Wüstenhimmel schwebenden Leuchtreklamen, die von den Besuchern umschwärmt wurden wie von Motten. Ein Quantensprung erfolgte 1958, als das Stardust die Nacht mit seiner 72 Meter langen und 9 Meter hohen Neongalaxie aus Kometen und Planeten zum Leuchten brachte.

Die Neonlichter zogen die Schaulustigen an, doch die Spieler brachten das Geld. Bis eine Polizeireform 1938 die Durchsetzung des Verbots von Glücksspiel und Prostitution in Hollywood erzwang, sah es dort ganz genauso aus wie später in Las Vegas. Gut gehende Spielkasinos reihten sich am Sunset Strip aneinander, kurz dahinter lagen für jedermann sichtbar die Bordelle; die Nachtclubs und Restaurants boten die höchsten kulinarischen Genüsse und die beste Unterhaltung im ganzen Land. Der Sunset Strip war eine Welt des Glamours, in der sich Filmstars und die Hollywood-Elite ein Stelldichein gaben. Als der Kandidat der Reformpartei Fletcher Bowron 1938 die Bürgermeisterwahl gewann und Glücksspiel und Prostitution aus L.A. verbannte, war es mit all dem schlagartig vorbei. Der große Kehraus zwang die Spieler L.A.s, sich auf die sechsstündige Reise in den einzigen Staat mit legalem Glücksspiel zu begeben. Wäre das Glücksspiel nicht 1938 in Kalifornien abgeschafft worden, wäre das Las Vegas, das wir heute kennen, nie entstanden.

## DIE ÄRA DER RESORTHOTELS (1941-1957)

Die Verwandlung von einer bescheidenen Wüstenoase zum gefragten Urlaubsziel geschah zu Beginn des Zweiten Weltkriegs. Spendierfreudige Soldaten des nahe gelegenen Luftwaffenstützpunkts tummelten sich in Las Vegas; die Armee drohte damit, Militärangehörigen den Zugang zur Stadt völlig zu verbieten, falls diese nichts gegen die Prostitution unternehme, die in ganz Las Vegas County dann fast zehn Jahre später tatsächlich verboten wurde. Das Glücksspiel blieb davon jedoch unbeeinflusst, die Gewinnmarge schnellte zwischen 1941 und 1944 um 56 Prozent in die Höhe. Las Vegas beschränkte sich nicht auf die Rolle als Scheidungsparadies Amerikas, sondern wurde auch zum Hochzeitsparadies. Allein 1942 wurden über 20 000 Heiratslizenzen im Clark County ausgestellt.

Am heute berühmten Las Vegas Strip wurde 1941 das erste Hotel gebaut. Der aus Los Angeles stammende Hotelmagnat Thomas Hull errichtete außerhalb der Stadtgrenze das El Rancho Vegas, eine Luxus-Ranch für reiche Städter, die nach heutigen Standards aber eher ein Motel als ein Resort war.

1946 wurde Hulls Konzept vom Resorthotel einen bedeutenden Schritt weiterentwickelt, als der aus Hollywood stammende Verleger und Restaurantbesitzer (und Vater des Autors) Billy Wilkerson ein Hotel baute und nach seinem Lieblingsvogel, dem Flamingo, benannte. Er wollte den Gästen mehr als eine Übernachtungsmöglichkeit und etwas Unterhaltung bieten und malte sich ein riesiges Spielerparadies mit 200 Zimmern aus, in dem Unterhaltung, Essen und Service vom Feinsten, noch dazu in europäischem Ambiente geboten werden sollten. Er entwarf die über 133 000 Quadratmeter große Anlage als ein in sich geschlossenes Universum, in dem die Besucher gar nicht erst auf die Idee kommen sollten, es verlassen zu wollen, wozu - geradezu revolutionär - der Einbau einer Klimaanlage entscheidend beitrug. Bis dahin waren die meisten Hotels nur mit elektrischen Deckenventilatoren, die die heiße Wüstenluft quirlten, oder mit primitiven Verdunstungskühlgeräten ausgestattet. Nun war die Wüste endlich bewohnbar. Wilkerson war es auch, der dem Strip in Anlehnung an den Sunset Boulevard seinen Namen gab. Seine Vorhersage, dass an dem staubigen Highway, an dem er baute, die Hotels eines Tages dicht an dicht stehen würden, sollte sich bewahrheiten.

Der Nachtclub-Impresario hatte allerdings einen schwerwiegenden Fehler: Er war ein besessener Spieler. Das Flamingo war erst halb fertig, als er das Geld zur Finanzierung am Spieltisch verlor. Ein Partner von Wilkerson war Bugsy Siegel, der nun die Kontrolle über das Bauvorhaben an sich reißen wollte. Als Wilkerson sich weigerte, die Zügel aus der Hand zu geben, bedrohte er ihn mit dem Tode. Und so floh Wilkerson nach Paris. Fünf Monate später, im Juni 1947, wurde der junge, bestechend gut aussehende Gangster Bugsy Siegel selbst erschossen.

Mit der Eröffnung von McCarran Field, dem einzigen Flughafen im Umkreis von Hunderten von Meilen, wurde Las Vegas 1948 auch für ausländische Touristen zum attraktiven Urlaubsziel. Die Stadt erlebte einen unglaublichen Zuwachs neuer Hotels, die zum größten Teil am Strip entstanden: das Desert Inn (1950), das Sahara und das Sands (1952), das Royal Nevada, das Dunes und das erste Hochhaus am Strip, das Riviera (1955), sowie das Hacienda (1956). Das Fremont (1956) in der Downtown war mit seinen 15 Stockwerken das höchste Gebäude Nevadas. Die Kosten für den Neubau eines Hotels stiegen explosionsartig von 5 Millionen Dollar Anfang der 50er Jahre auf 15 Millionen Dollar, die der Bau des Tropicana 1957 bereits verschlang. Die Anzahl der

Zimmer nahm ebenfalls zu, von 300 zu Beginn des Jahrzehnts auf 1000, so etwa im Stardust von 1958. Die Hotels fingen an, grandiose Themen zu entwickeln und auszubauen. Das arabische Motiv des Dunes zum Beispiel gab den Ton für die überladenen Zuckerbäckerbauten vor, die sich später am Strip den Rang streitig machten. Die Riesenresorts waren aus Las Vegas nicht mehr wegzudenken.

### DIE ENTERTAINMENT-ÄRA (1958-1965)

In den 50ern wurde Las Vegas zum Inbegriff des Showbusiness. Berühmte Stars wie Frank Sinatra oder Judy Garland hatten ihre ersten Auftritte in Las Vegas. Der Sänger, der später zum größten Publikumsmagneten in der Geschichte von Las Vegas werden sollte, stieß anfangs ironischerweise auf wenig Begeisterung – den Frank-Sinatra-Fans sagte Elvis Presleys frivoler Hüftschwung 1958 noch nicht zu.

Doch auch im prosperierenden Las Vegas der späten 50er, frühen 60er gab es Konfliktpotenzial. Schwarze Künstler waren zwar als Entertainer beliebt, die Benutzung der Hotelanlagen blieb ihnen jedoch verwehrt. 1958 verweigerten sie die Unterzeichnung aller weiteren Verträge, wenn die Hotels nicht auch für sie geöffnet würden. Hinter der glitzernden Fassade befehdeten sich die Gangster, die in ihren Hotels die Kontrolle über die Auftritte der Stars hatten, ganz zu schweigen von abgekarteten Glücksspielen, von Drogen, illegaler Prostitution und nicht minder illegalen Boxkämpfen. Überirdische Atomtests, die an der Nevada Test Site nordwestlich von Las Vegas durchgeführt wurden, waren den Hotelbesitzern beständig ein Dorn im Auge, weil geschäftsschädigend.

Das Jahrzehnt endete positiv mit der eher zufälligen Entstehung des Superstar-Entertainments am Strip. Während der Dreharbeiten zum Warner-Brothers-Klassiker *Ocean's Eleven* (dt. Titel *Frankie und seine Spießgesellen*) übernahmen Peter Lawford, Frank Sinatra, Dean Martin, Sammy Davis Jr. und Joey Bishop ab dem 20. Januar 1960 drei Wochen lang die Bühne im Sands und veranstalteten wilde Partys, die tagtäglich bis in die frühen Morgenstunden dauerten. Die Presse nannte es „Das Gipfeltreffen im Sands", doch die Entertainer gingen schlicht unter dem Namen „The Rat Pack" in die Geschichte ein.

# DIE ÄRA DER THEMEN-HOTELS (1966-1979)

Mitte der 6oer Jahre wechselte Las Vegas wieder einmal den Besitzer. Wenn Billy Wilkersons Flamingo Hotel der Magnet gewesen war, der die Mafiapaten scharenweise in die Stadt gelockt hatte, dann war der pressescheue Wirtschaftsmagnat Howard Hughes der Kameltreiber, der sie in die Wüste schickte. Während seiner vier Jahre in Las Vegas wurde er zum größten Immobilienbesitzer der Stadt. Unter Hughes' Ägide entstand das Konzept von Las Vegas als Ferienziel für die ganze Familie, das mit der Eröffnung des Caesars Palace 1966 und des Circus Circus 1968 erstmals umgesetzt wurde. Während der 7oer wurden die Hotels immer riesiger. Das 1972 eröffnete MGM Grand hatte schon 2 100 Zimmer.

13 Jahre nach seinem ersten erfolglosen Revueauftritt feierte Elvis Presley seine triumphale Rückkehr nach Las Vegas und verdiente die höchsten Gagen in der Geschichte der Stadt.

# DIE ÄRA DER KONZERNE (1980-2000)

Die Fließbandproduktion von Autos lief 1917 in Dearborn, Michigan, in der River-Rouge-Fabrik von Henry Ford an. Von den 8oer Jahren an ahmte Las Vegas das Vorbild der Automobilherstellung nach und verwandelte sich in eine einzige Unterhaltungsindustrie. Trotz Hughes' früheren Vorstößen wurde Las Vegas erst jetzt wirklich als Ikone der amerikanischen Popkultur anerkannt. Die Hotels zählten jetzt nicht mehr 2 000, sondern 3 000 Zimmer und boten in ihren Anlagen von wilden Tieren bis zu riesigen Achterbahnen einfach alles. Im Jahr 2000 gaben sich bereits mehr als 120 000 Paare das Jawort in Vegas.

Viele ältere Hotels strengten sich nun mächtig an, um den Anschluss nicht zu verlieren. 1982 fand nach einer 25-Millionen-Dollar-Schönheitsoperation die Neueröffnung des alten Thunderbird als neues El Rancho statt. Im Jahre 1986 schnellten die Besucherzahlen rasant in die Höhe; allein in den ersten elf Monaten wurden 14,2 Millionen Touristen gezählt, was andere Hotels wie das Aladdin dazu verleitete, ebenfalls Hals über Kopf zu modernisieren.

Die Ära der Konzerne hielt mit dem Getränkegroßhändler Steve Wynn Einzug, der bei einem Immobiliengeschäft gehörig abgesahnt hatte und seinen Gewinn in das gigantische, eine halbe Milliarde Dollar teure Mirage steckte. Das Grundstück nimmt 350 000 Quadratmeter am Strip ein; das Hotel mit seinen 3 303 Gästezimmern ist bis heute das weltweit größte Hotel in Privatbesitz geblieben. Als das Mirage 1989 eröffnete, waren die Würfel für die Zukunft der Hotels in Las Vegas gefallen. Eine Phase hektischer Baumaßnahmen folgte. In deren Folge eröffneten das Excalibur (1990), das Luxor und das Treasure Island mit jeweils mehr als 2 000 Zimmern sowie der neu gestaltete Freizeitpark des MGM (1993). Das Stratosphere mit dem höchsten Aussichtsturm Amerikas eröffnete 1996. Es folgten das New York-New York (1997), das Bellagio (1998) sowie die Hotels Venetian, Mandalay Bay und Paris Las Vegas (1999). Mit dem mondänen Bellagio, vor dem die Landschaft am Comer See stilvoll nachempfunden wurde, traf Wynn den Geschmack der Zeit. Das 36 Stockwerke hohe Resorthotel mit seinem 34 000 Quadratmeter großen See wurde zum Treffpunkt der echten Spieler, die sich im Gewühl der Kinderbelustigungen nicht mehr wohl fühlten.

Diese rasante Entwicklung hatte allerdings ihren Preis. Für die atemberaubenden Ausblicke auf Vulkane und Schlösser, europäische Hauptstädte und Piratenschiffe musste Platz geschaffen werden; die Hotels Dunes, Sands und Hacienda wurden abgerissen, damit sich neue Bauten aus ihrem Staub erheben konnten.

Las Vegas wurde nie am Reißbrett geplant. Das Bemerkenswerte an der Stadt ist, dass sie sich immer wieder völlig neu erfindet. Ihre Entwicklungsgeschichte ist ein Patchwork aus Fehlern, Experimenten, pragmatischen Lösungen und chaotischen Visionen, die in den Jahren seit 1931 zu einem Bestand von 130 000 Zimmern geführt haben, die dicht an dicht an einem nicht einmal sechs Kilometer langen Stück Highway liegen, dort, wo vor nicht allzu langer Zeit noch menschenleere Wüste war. 7,2 Milliarden Dollar Einnahmen aus dem Glücksspiel und 36 Millionen Touristen im Jahr – sie verdanken sich dem Glauben ans geschenkte Geld des Glücksspiels, der Las Vegas zur amerikanischen Konsum-, Kapitalismus- und Kitsch-Metropole gemacht hat.

# VIVA LAS VEGAS

IL N'Y A PAS SI LONGTEMPS ENCORE, CE N'ÉTAIT QU'UNE PETITE VILLE FRONTIÈRE POUSSIÉREUSE, ABRITANT QUELQUES MODESTES SALLES DE JEUX ET PEUPLÉE DE PERSONNAGES QUI SEMBLAIENT ÊTRE SORTIS TOUT DROIT D'UN VIEUX WESTERN. DEPUIS, ELLE EST DEVENUE LA VILLE DU VICE, UN UNIVERS DE NÉONS OÙ LE JEU ET LA PROSTITUTION FONT BON MÉNAGE. POUR ASSURER SON FONCTIONNEMENT : LA MÉCANIQUE BIEN HUILÉE DU CRIME ORGANISÉ, ET LA PRODUCTION DU DIVERTISSE-MENT DE MASSE À UN NIVEAU INTERNATIONAL. ELLE FUT LA PREMIÈRE À DEVENIR UN SYMBOLE AMÉRICAIN DU PARC À THÈMES. CETTE VILLE, CONNUE DU MONDE ENTIER, A POUR NOM LAS VEGAS.

## LA NOUVELLE FRONTIÈRE (1829-1930)

Un jeune éclaireur du nom de Rafael Rivera fut, en 1829, le premier à pénétrer sur le territoire. Il y découvrit des sources qu'il baptisa Las Vegas, un nom peu adéquat, puis-qu'il signifie en espagnol « les prairies ». L'endroit peut en effet se targuer d'avoir l'un des climats les plus extrêmes d'Amérique du Nord. Ici, la chaleur accablante des mois d'été peut battre des records, et en hiver, il n'est pas rare qu'il y gèle à pierre fendre. À l'époque, la traversée du désert du Mojave était une véritable aventure, et une rude épreuve pour les voyageurs qui se rendaient sur la côte.

En 1844, le pionnier John C. Fremont conduisit une expédition militaire américaine à Las Vegas pour dresser la carte du territoire. Ces hommes n'y restèrent pas longtemps. Dix ans plus tard, une trentaine de missionnaires mormons venus de l'Utah y édifièrent un fort. Celui-ci devait assurer la protection d'une route postale, décidée par le Congrès, entre Salt Lake City et San Diego. Mais des années de conditions de vie éprouvantes, de querelles internes et un raid indien en 1857 les poussèrent à regagner Salt Lake.

C'est finalement la voie ferrée qui créa Las Vegas, qui transforma ce nulle part en une localité digne de ce nom. En 1862, le Congrès adopta une charte autorisant l'Union Pacific Railroad à établir une liaison avec la ligne de la Central Pacific Railroad à la frontière californienne. Las Vegas, Nevada (reconnu comme un État en 1864), fut offi-ciellement fondée le 15 mai 1905 lorsque l'on posa le dernier rail sur le sol du désert. Les voyageurs se rendant sur la côte californienne purent désormais traverser le désert beaucoup plus rapidement qu'à cheval ou en chariot.

Les promoteurs et entrepreneurs en tout genre ne tardèrent pas à s'intéresser à Las Vegas. Le premier hôtel important, un établissement de 30 chambres avec un auvent en toile, baptisé Hotel Las Vegas, ouvrit bientôt pour les affaires. Deux ans plus tard, en 1907, les premiers lampadaires électriques firent leur apparition sur Fremont Street. Ils étaient alimentés par un moteur à un cylindre de 90 chevaux nommé Old Betsy. L'économie qui se mit en place était typique du Far West. Chevaux et troupeaux de bétail demeurèrent dans la vallée tout au long des années 30, et même après que des puits artésiens y eurent été découverts, celle-ci ne devint jamais une région agricole.

Le jeu, la prostitution et le débit d'alcool étaient légaux depuis la fondation de l'État. En 1906, cependant, ils furent circonscrits à une zone bruyante du nord de la ville, le quartier chaud connu sous le nom de « Block 16 », et du premier établissement de luxe de Las Vegas, l'Arizona Club.

En 1910, la ville fit un grand pas en arrière en matière de législation. Sous la pression des ligues pour les droits des femmes et contre le jeu, les législateurs de l'État votèrent l'interdiction de toutes les formes de jeu. Bien qu'illégale, la pratique fut encore tolérée à condition d'être reléguée dans les arrière-salles des bars et des clubs. Comprenant que l'avenir de la ville ne dépendait pas du chemin de fer mais de l'automobile, Las Vegas dépensa 10 000 dollars pour construire la route vers Jean (à côté de la voie ferrée de l'État) qui fut l'amorce de la Route 91. En 1925, toutes les rues du sud de la ville étaient pavées, et moins de vingt ans après, les hôtels allaient construire de vastes parkings pour accueillir les automobilistes.

## L'ÈRE DE LA SCIURE (1931-1940)

Loin d'être à l'époque une destination touristique, le Nevada, dont l'économie était vacillante, avait besoin d'un coup de fouet. Ce fut en 1931 qu'il se vit offrir les trois cadeaux qui allaient valoir à Las Vegas d'être indiquée sur la carte des États-Unis. Tout d'abord, le Boulder Canyon Project Act, que le président des États-Unis Calvin Coolidge avait signé en 1928, prévoyait la construction du plus grand barrage au monde pour un coût de près de 49 millions de dollars. Le but du Hoover Dam, ou barrage Hoover, situé à une cinquantaine de kilomètres de Las Vegas, était de fournir de l'électricité à l'Ouest et de surmonter la Dépression. Ce qui fut le plus grand projet de construction de l'histoire américaine amena des milliers d'ouvriers. Le deuxième cadeau arriva en mars : le gouverneur Fred Balzar signa une « autorisation de jeu illimitée » qui fit du Nevada le premier État de l'Union à adopter la pratique légale du jeu. Enfin, la législation sur le divorce devint la plus libérale du pays, lorsque le délai minimum de résidence fut réduit de trois mois à six semaines.

Las Vegas connut alors un véritable boom. Les baraques en bois d'un étage cédèrent la place aux structures en briques de deux étages, et la ville eut pour trophée l'Apache Hotel, un bâtiment de trois étages et d'une centaine de chambres construit en 1932. Les casinos fleurirent le long de Fremont Street, un secteur connu sous le nom de « Ravin Éclatant ». La population appelait les casinos des « boîtes à sciure », à cause de celle qui était répandue sur le sol. Avec de nouveaux trottoirs et de nouvelles boutiques, Las Vegas apparaissait de plus en plus comme le Main Street des États-Unis, avec une différence notable cependant : le jeu en était le première ressource économique.

L'Histoire attribue à Tom Hull l'idée d'abriter un night-club, un casino et un hôtel sous le même toit dans son établissement ouvert en 1941 : El Rancho Vegas. Ce concept était en fait le fruit des cogitations d'une célèbre figure de la pègre de Los Angeles, Tony Cornero, qui le 2 mai 1931 avait ouvert le Meadows Club sur Boulder Highway. L'Histoire voudrait également nous faire croire que le crime organisé s'est installé à Las Vegas en 1946 avec Benjamin « Bugsy » Siegel, le gangster de Los Angeles, alors que Cornero avait en fait déjà étendu son influence dans le sud du Nevada, annonçant la mainmise du crime sur la ville.

En 1934, la ville reçut un autre cadeau : le néon. Arrivé de Paris, il illumina en premier le grand auvent du Boulder Club. Les lumières colorées se multiplièrent dans le ciel du désert et, année après année, attiraient les visiteurs comme une lanterne les phalènes. La vogue du néon au milieu des années 40 conquit aussi le cow-boy du Pioneer Club, sur Fremont Street, et les enseignes des clubs Las Vegas et Monte Carlo. La féérie lumineuse atteignit un nouveau palier en 1958, lorsque le Stardust illumina la nuit avec sa galaxie en néon de comètes et de planètes, de 72 mètres de long et 9 mètres de haut.

Si les lumières attiraient les spectateurs, c'était le jeu qui faisait venir les flambeurs. Jusqu'en 1938, et la mise en vigueur d'une réforme condamnant plus sévèrement le jeu et la prostitution, Hollywood possédait bien avant l'avènement de Las Vegas tout qui faisait la réputation de celle-ci. Des casinos florissants tels que le Clover Club et le Colony ponctuaient le Sunset Strip, les bordels se cachaient un peu à l'écart des artères principales, et les night-clubs et les restaurants offraient une nourriture exquise et ce qui se faisait de mieux en matière de divertissement dans le pays. Le Sunset Strip était un univers séduisant où se rassemblaient les stars de cinéma et le gratin de Hollywood. Tout changea pourtant lorsqu'en 1938, Fletcher Bowron remporta les élections municipales et mit fin au jeu et à la prostitution à L.A. Seuls furent épargnés les champs de course, tel Santa Anita. Le grand nettoyage obligea les joueurs à affronter les six heures de voyage en voiture (sans climatisation) vers le seul État où le jeu était légal. La route était alors dépourvue de boutiques et de stations-service et de nombreux voyageurs emportaient des jerricans d'essence dans leur coffre. Sans l'interdiction du jeu en Californie, Las Vegas, telle que nous la connaissons, n'aurait jamais existé.

## L'ÈRE DE L'HÔTELLERIE (1941-1957)

La transformation de Las Vegas de modeste oasis en pôle touristique remonte aux premières semaines de l'entrée en guerre des États-Unis. Les ouvriers de la Défense américaine, stationnés sur la base aérienne toute proche, débarquaient à Las Vegas, impatients de dépenser leur argent. L'armée menaça d'interdire l'accès de la ville au personnel militaire s'il n'était pas mis fin à la prostitution. Une dizaine d'années plus tard, le Comté finit par en proscrire la pratique (on peut cependant toujours visiter Pahrump, Nevada, à une heure de là, pour profiter en toute légalité du sexe tarifé). Le jeu, quant à lui, conserva tout son pouvoir, et les recettes augmentèrent de cinquante-six pour cent entre 1941 et 1944. Non contente d'être la capitale du divorce, Las Vegas devint également celle du mariage. En 1942, plus de vint mille certificats de publication de bans furent délivrés par le Comté de Clark, mariages dont la plupart étaient célébrés dans des petites chapelles du bord de route.

Le célèbre Las Vegas Strip vit le jour en 1941, en dehors de la ville, avec le El Rancho Vegas de Thomas Hull, magnat de l'hôtellerie. El Rancho qui avait été conçu comme un ranch de luxe, mais selon les critères d'aujourd'hui, ressemblerait davantage à un motel qu'à un complexe hôtelier. Hull comprit le potentiel touristique de la ville et fit bâtir son hôtel directement sur la Route 91, un secteur du Comté de Clark où les taxes étaient bien moins élevées et les règles de construction beaucoup plus souples.

En 1946, l'éditeur et restaurateur hollywoodien (et père de l'auteur) Billy Wilkerson affina le concept touristique de Hull et baptisa son hôtel du nom de Flamingo, son oiseau favori. Soucieux d'offrir à ses clients davantage qu'un lit et un peu de distraction, il conçut un établissement de deux cents chambres avec des attractions de première classe, et une nourriture et un service à l'européenne. Il nicha son paradis dans une quinzaine d'hectares, de manière à ce que le visiteur n'ait pas envie d'en repartir – le système révolutionnaire de climatisation y étant aussi pour quelque chose. Jusqu'alors en effet, la plupart des hôtels n'étaient équipés que de ventilateurs électriques au plafond qui brassaient l'air brûlant du désert. Le pari de Wilkerson sur l'air climatisé rendit enfin le désert habitable. Ce fut également Wilkerson qui baptisa le Strip d'après celui de Sunset Boulevard, Strip le long duquel s'alignaient ses nightclubs et ses restaurants à succès, tels les Ciro's et La Rue's. De fait, il ne s'était pas trompé en prédisant que la route poussiéreuse sur laquelle il faisait construire serait un jour bordée d'hôtels de bout en bout.

Le constructeur de night-clubs avait cependant un défaut fatal : la passion du jeu. Il n'avait achevé que la moitié du Flamingo lorsqu'il perdit les fonds de la construction sur les tapis verts. Wilkerson était associé à Bugsy Siegel, habitué à faire parler les armes, et qui exigeait davantage de contrôle sur le projet. Siegel menaça Wilkerson de mort lorsque celui-ci se refusa à lâcher les rênes. La menace étant sérieuse, Wilkerson s'enfuit à Paris pour sauver sa vie. Cinq mois plus tard, en juin 1947, le jeune et beau gangster était abattu au domicile de sa compagne, Virginia Hill, qui avait été elle aussi contrainte de se réfugier à Paris.

Avec l'ouverture en 1948 du McCarran Field, le seul aéroport à des centaines de kilomètres à la ronde, Las Vegas devint une destination touristique internationale. La ville connut un nouveau boom immobilier. La plupart des nouveaux hôtels furent construits sur le Strip : le Desert Inn (1950), le Sahara and Sands (1952), le Royal Nevada, le Dunes et le Riviera (1955), première construction en hauteur, et l'Hacienda (1956). Le Fremont (1956), hôtel de quinze étages situé dans le quartier sud de la ville, était la plus haute construction du Nevada. Le coût de construction des hôtels augmenta de façon vertigineuse, passant de 5 millions de dollars au début des années 1950 à 15 millions avec la construction du Tropicana en 1957. Le nombre de chambres augmenta également, passant de trois cents au début de la décennie au millier offert par le Stardust en 1958. Les hôtels commencèrent à se développer et à proposer des thèmes grandioses. Le style arabe des Dunes, par exemple, ouvrit la voie aux constructions kitsch qui plus tard peuplèrent le Strip. L'idée d'offrir le superlatif s'était définitivement implantée.

## L'ÈRE DU SPECTACLE (1958-1965)

Au cours des années 50, Las Vegas devint également synonyme de spectacle. De nombreuses stars, de Frank Sinatra à Judy Garland, vinrent éclairer et animer la scène de Las Vegas, pour la première fois au cours de cette décennie. La ville accueillit de luxueuses productions telles que le Lido de Paris et Les Folies Bergère. Ironie du sort, le chanteur qui allait devenir la plus grande vedette de toute l'histoire du spectacle à Las Vegas, commença par y faire un flop. En 1956, le déhanchement et la voix rauque d'Elvis Presley échouèrent à chauffer la salle avant le set de Sinatra.

La Las Vegas prospère de la fin des années 50 et du début des années 60 n'échappait pas à la controverse. Les artistes noirs, bien que jouant un rôle central sur une scène artistique florissante, étaient toujours interdits dans les hôtels, et en 1958 ils refusèrent de signer tout contrat tant que cette interdiction ne serait pas levée. Derrière le tape-à-l'œil, opéraient les bandes de gangsters qui dictaient leurs ordres aux artistes se produisant dans leurs hôtels, pour ne rien dire des jeux truqués, de la prostitution et des combats de boxe illégaux. Les essais nucléaires dans l'atmosphère, effectués sur le Nevada Test Site au nord-ouest de Las Vegas, étaient un souci perpétuel pour les directeurs d'hôtels qui prétendaient que le fait d'apercevoir des champignons atomiques depuis leurs établissements était mauvais pour les affaires.

La décennie s'acheva sur une note positive avec la naissance sur le Strip d'un spectacle de superstars qui survint presque par hasard. Le 20 janvier 1960, durant le tournage du film *L'Inconnu de Las Vegas*, Peter Lawford, Frank Sinatra, Dean Martin, Sammy Davis Jr. et Joey Bishop investirent pendant trois semaines la scène du Sands pour présenter un grand show qui durait jusqu'au petit matin. La presse présenta l'événement comme la «rencontre au sommet du Sands», mais les artistes furent immortalisés sans façons sous le nom de «Rat Pack».

## L'ÈRE THÉMATIQUE (1966-1979)

Au milieu des années 60, Las Vegas évolua dans une nouvelle direction. Si l'hôtel Flamingo de Billy Wilkerson fit bon accueil au crime organisé, Howard Hughes, le fameux magnat des affaires qui aimait vivre en reclus, fut l'éclaireur qui ouvrit une nouvelle voie. Durant les quatre années de son règne, il s'empara du Frontier, du Desert Inn, du Sands, du Silver Slipper, du Landmark et du Castaways, remportant le titre de plus gros propriétaire de Las Vegas. C'est à cette époque que l'idée vint d'attirer les familles à Las Vegas, concrétisée par l'ouverture du Caesars Palace en 1966 et du Circus Circus en 1968. Les hôtels se firent plus hauts et plus vastes encore au cours des années 70. Le MGM Grand, baptisé du nom du studio hollywoodien qui l'avait fait construire, ouvrit en 1972 avec 2100 chambres.

Treize ans après ses malheureux débuts au cabaret, Elvis Presley fit un retour triomphal à Las Vegas, devenant le plus gros salarié de l'histoire de la ville.Lorsque le King se produisait sur scène, les rentrées des hôtels et des casinos sur le Strip augmentaient en moyenne de dix pour cent, et jusqu'à aujourd'hui aucun artiste n'a relevé ce défi.

## L'ÈRE DE LA GRANDE ENTREPRISE (1980-2000)

C'est en 1917 à Dearborn, Michigan, dans l'usine de River Rouge créée par Henry Ford, que débuta la construction en série des automobiles. Au cours des années 80, Las Vegas prit exemple sur le constructeur automobile pour mettre sur pied une gigantesque chaîne de production entièrement dédiée au divertissement. En dépit des premières tentatives de Hughes, ce n'est pas avant cette période que Las Vegas fit figure d'icône de la culture populaire américaine. Le nombre de chambres par hôtel grimpa de deux mille à trois mille et les terrains de ces hôtels accueillirent aussi bien des animaux exotiques que des montagnes russes à thèmes. Depuis 2000, plus de cent vingt mille couples viennent s'y marier chaque année.

De nombreux hôtels plus anciens fermèrent pour se transformer. En 1982, le vieux Thunderbird rouvrit sous le nom de El Rancho après un lifting de 25 millions de dollars. Las Vegas connut une année phénoménale en 1986, avec un chiffre record de 14,2 millions de visiteurs dans les onze premiers mois, ce qui incita d'autres hôtels tels que l'Aladdin à se transformer en toute hâte.

L'ère de la grande entreprise ne commença vraiment qu'avec l'intervention du distributeur d'alcool Steve Wynn, qui se lança dans un pari immobilier et engloutit tous ses profits dans le Mirage, un mammouth d'un demi-milliard de dollars. Couvrant une quarantaine d'hectares du Strip et disposant de 3303 chambres, il demeure le plus grand hôtel du monde. Wynn apporta ainsi la preuve que les joueurs préféraient un décor attrayant aux espaces bruyants et congestionnés des autres hôtels. Le Mirage, ouvert en 1989, laissait présager l'avenir des hôtels à Las Vegas. Suivit une période de construction effrénée, aboutissant à l'Excalibur (1990), au Louxor et au Treasure Island, chacun dépassant les deux mille chambres, et à la rénovation du parc à thèmes du Grand Hotel (1993).Puis le Stratosphère (1996) qui se vantait d'être la plus haute tour d'observation aux États-Unis, le New York-New York (1997), le Bellagio (1998) ainsi que le Venetian, le Mandalay Bay et le Paris Las Vegas (1999) ouvrirent leurs portes. Wynn visa juste avec l'élégant Bellagio (ce mot signifiant «relaxation élégante» en italien), inspiré par le lac de Côme. Le bâtiment de trente-six étages, doté d'un lac de quatre hectares, attira les joueurs authentiques qui se sentaient auparavant perdus au milieu des divertissements familiaux.

Le prix à payer pour ce développement fut un sacrifice historique. Il fallait libérer de l'espace pour le fascinant panorama des volcans et des châteaux, des capitales européennes et des aventures de pirates, et le Dunes, le Sands et l'Hacienda furent tous démolis afin de permettre à de nouvelles constructions de s'élever sur leurs décombres.

Las Vegas ne connut jamais de développement planifié. La ville est remarquable pour sa capacité à changer régulièrement de peau et à se réinventer. Son évolution est une succession d'erreurs, d'expérimentations, de solutions pratiques et de visions chaotiques qui ont depuis 1931 donné lieu à la création de 130 000 chambres, alignées le long d'une route de six kilomètres et demi qui n'était auparavant qu'un bout de désert. Las Vegas peut se vanter par ailleurs de 7,2 milliards de dollars annuels de bénéfices apportés par le jeu et de trente six millions de touristes par an – tous réunis par la philosophie du «tout-pour-rien» du casino, et qui font d'elle la capitale de la consommation, du capitalisme et du kitsch américain.

# THE STRIP

TRAVELODGE

STARDUST HOTEL

CIRCUS CIRCUS

SILVER SLIPPER

FRONTIER HOTEL

FRONTIER

ALEX LEE PRESENTS
EDDIE FISHER
MUSICAL DIRECTOR EDDY MANSON
JOEY FORMAN
BALLET AMERICA

JACK E LEONARD
JIMMIE RODGERS

THE MINT

FREMONT HOTEL

RIVERIA

SAHARA

DESERT INN HOTEL

*Landmark Hotel*
*Las Vegas,*
*Nevada*

# Stay where the Stars Play
## Play where the Stars Stay

Daringly creative . . . romantically imaginative. Breaking every precedent, the Hotel Sahara has paved a star-studded highway to the top of the entertainment setting a unique pattern which—although imitated—has never been equalled.

...ssing through the mystic portals to discover a chapter from the land of Fable . . . an enchanting Mecca designed to capture your every sense with delightful ingredients for a memorable adventure . . . You'll subtly sense that ...ve embarked upon a timeless vacation where endless fascination beckons you on all sides.

Lyrical moments . . . gentle magic . . . for here is the chosen rendezvous of the show world's most celebrated personalities and the hotel world's most pampered guests.

SAHARA

Telephone
6800

HIWAY 91
LAS VEGAS, NEV.

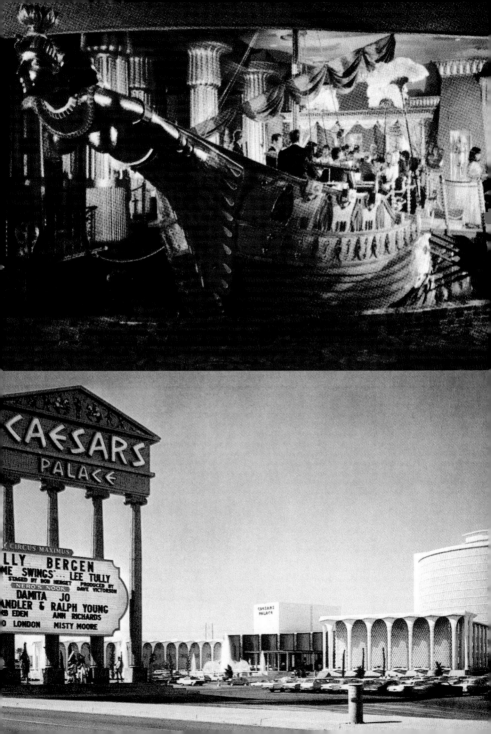

# DOWNTOWN

Largest Sign
West of Chicago

VEGAS
BINGO
JACK POT
ARCADE

LAS VEGAS CLUB
CK POT ARCADE · RACE HORSE BETTING · COCKTAILS

Thunderbird
HOTEL

The MINT
DOWNTOWN
LAS VEGAS, NEVA

Horseshoe

APACHE HOTEL
LAS VEGAS
NEVADA

Eldorado
CLUB

GOLDEN NUGGET

GOLDEN
NUGGET

GAMBLING HOUSE

GOLDEN NUGGET
GAMBLING HALL
1905
RESTAURANT
SALOON
BOB WILLS
CASINO
GOLDEN NUGGET
GOLDEN NUGGET

# GAMBLING

# ROULE

## *Gaming* GU

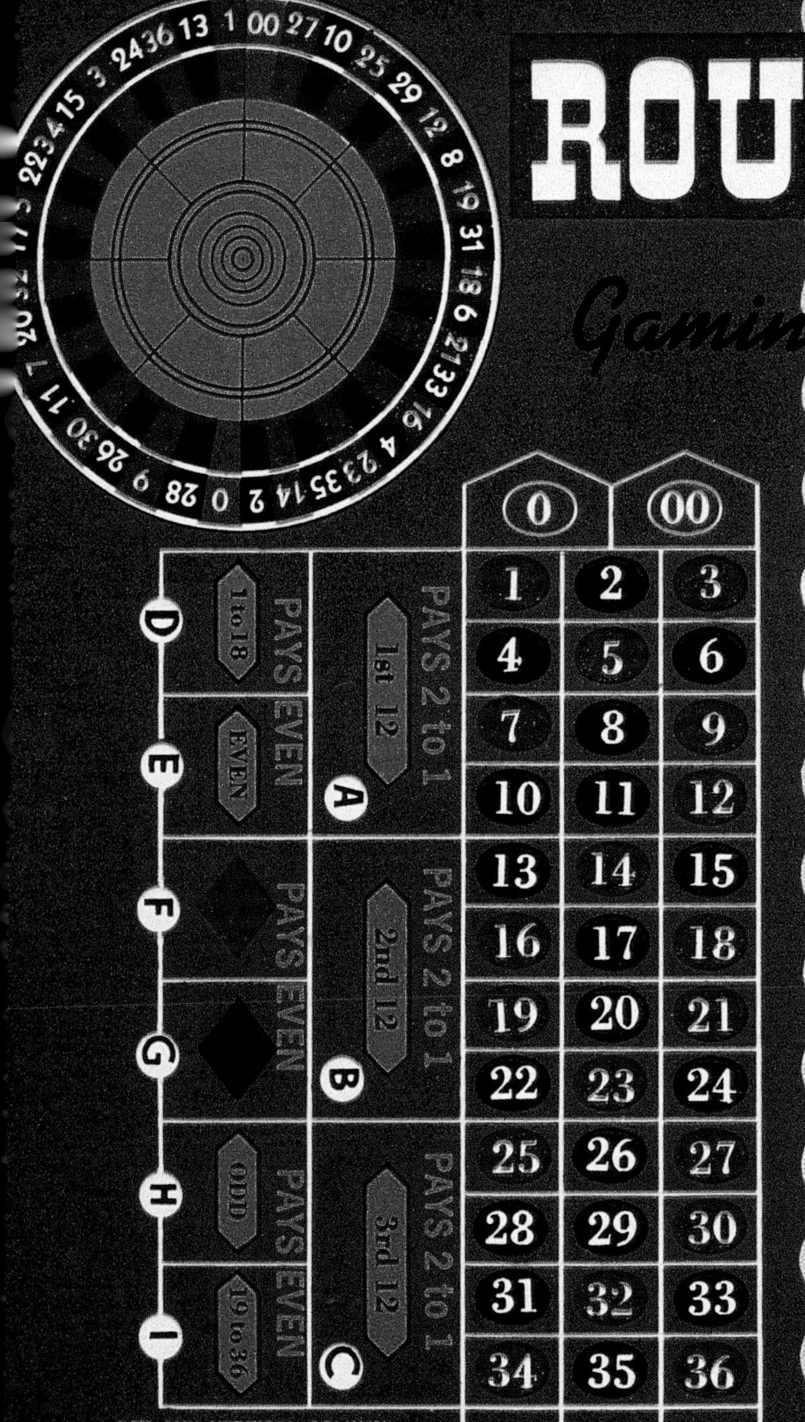


BET ANY VERTICAL COLUMN

BE
RED or
"F" or
AS ILLUS
PAYS

BE
EVEN o
"E" or
AS ILLUS
PAYS

BET 19
"I
AS ILLUS
PAYS

BET 1
"D
AS ILLUS
PAYS

BET 25
3rd 1
"C
AS ILLU
PAYS

Greetings from *Las Vegas* Nevada

# LOUNGE ACTS

# XAVIER CUGAT

AND HIS ORCHESTRA

featuring ABBE LANE

NEXT ATTRACTION

GUY MITCHELL MARY McCARTY

CURRENTLY APPEARING

# SHELLEY WINTERS

Extra Added Attraction!

## JACKIE KANNON

FOUR RAMSES

A SEYMOUR FELIX PRODUCTION

A NEW HIGH
IN RESORT
LIVING!

HOTEL
SAHARA

FEATURING . . .

the Painted Desert Room
AMERICA'S SMARTEST SUPPER CLUB . . . .
Presents . . . .
Wilbur Clark's
DESERT INN

# Folies Bergere!

## DIRECT FROM PARIS—EXCLUSIVE AT HOTEL TROPICANA IN LAS VEGAS!

EARL GRANT

JOE E. LEWIS

JACK CARTER

BOBBY DARIN

MYRON COHEN

BILLY EC

Nowhe
p

LAS VEGAS, NEVADA

HOTEL SAHARA

LAS V

HOTEL SA

*Folies Bergere*

AMERICAN HOME
THE Tropicana HOTEL
OF THE FOLIES BERGERE

LAS VEGAS

# *Royal Nevada*

## HOTEL
## LAS VEGAS, NEVADA

FOR *Royal*

ENTERTAINMENT

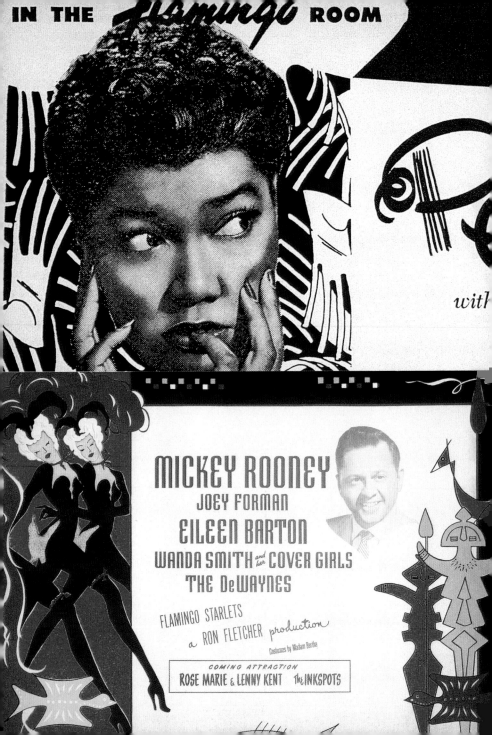

IN THE *Flamingo* ROOM

with

MICKEY ROONEY
JOEY FORMAN
EILEEN BARTON
WANDA SMITH and her COVER GIRLS
THE DeWAYNES

FLAMINGO STARLETS
a RON FLETCHER production
Costumes by Madam Bertha

COMING ATTRACTION
ROSE MARIE & LENNY KENT   The INKSPOTS

# BOOZE AND BUFFETS

Painted Desert
Room

Wilbur Clark's
DESERT INN
LAS VEGAS NEVADA

Menu

OF THIS WORLD!

MENU

NEW FRONTIER HOTEL

LAS VEGAS

As an
example of
Out-Of-The-World
Fare in
Entertainment...

Our Famous
CHINESE
MENU

The Sands

IN THE HICKORY ROOM AT THE *Riviera* LAS VEGAS

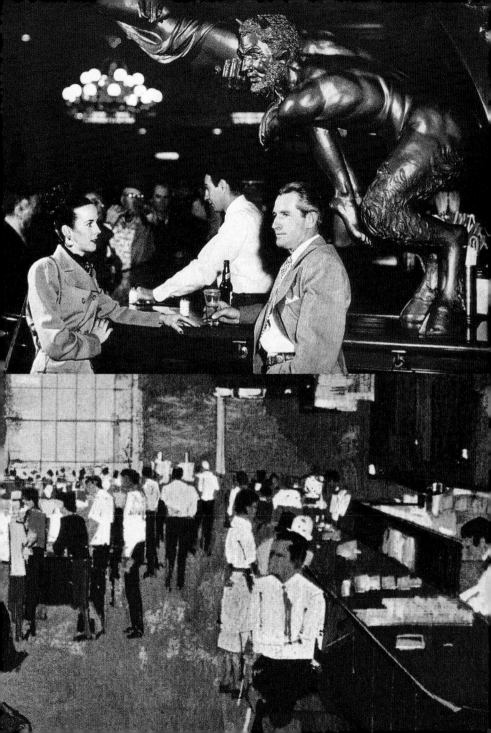

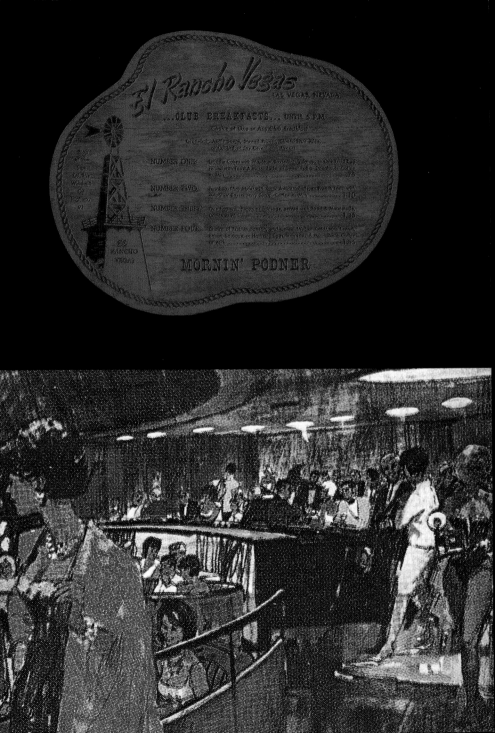

THE Flamingo HOTEL

LAS VEGAS, NEVADA

THE WORLD'S FINEST RESORT HOTEL

Greetings from
The Desert Inn

MY KIND OF TOWN

# Las Vegas
### BROADWAY OF THE DESERT

PLAY AROUND THE CLOCK
LAS VEGAS NEVADA

## A Whirl of Fun
## and EXCITEMENT!

Nowhere in the world can you find such fun and excitement. Relax under the friendly Nevada sky during the day and visit the fascinating casinos at night. The clock never stops and the doors never close in this resort haven whose welcome is "Howdy Podner, come as you are."..... See the nation's top entertainers..... enjoy excellent food at the dinner shows... colorful buffet served from midnight to dawn... fine cuisine at the exotic restaurants... lavish swimming pools at hotels, motels and guest ranches... horseback riding through the scenic desert... fishing and boating on nearby Lake Mead... golfing at two of the nation's finest 18-hole courses... dancing to the music of famous bands... Fremont Street, known as the "Gay White Way of the West" and "The World's Largest Gambling Center"... the world renowned Strip with its multi-million dollar hotels and entertainment... top name musical combos at intimate cocktail lounges, from dusk to dawn........ state regulated gaming... complete convention facilities ... ideal climate with 99 percent sunshine and low humidity the year round... marriage license bureau and wedding chapels open 24 hours a day.... Hollywood stars at play... All this and more await you in Las Vegas, Nevada, the FUN AND ENTERTAINMENT CAPITAL OF THE WORLD.

CONVENTION

GOLDEN NUGGET

from STE

Nevada

● SAN FRANCISCO

California

LAS VEGA

LOS ANGELES ●

# There's always something going on in LAS VEGAS!

## The Fabulous Resort Hotel Strip

### Hotel LAST FRONTIER · FLAMINGO · EL RANCHO
### THUNDERBIRD · DESERT INN · SAHARA

25c

# Fabulous
## LAS VEGAS *Magazine*

©

Don't forget....
V.F.W.

"Poppy
Days"

Nov. 7th thru 11th

JACK CORTEZ *Fabulous* LAS VEGAS
*magazine*
every

# 1945  LAS VEGAS  1945

# HELLDORADO

## SOUVENIR ANNUAL

# LAS VEGAS FROM 1829-1999

**1829**  Scout discovers springs in the desert and names surrounding area Las Vegas.

Scout entdeckt Quellen in der Wüste und nennt die Gegend Las Vegas.

Un éclaireur découvre des sources dans le désert et baptise l'endroit « Las Vegas ».

**1844**  Civilian pathfinder John C. Fremont leads expedition to Las Vegas and maps the territory.

Pfadfinder John C. Fremont leitet eine Expedition nach Las Vegas und vermisst das Land.

Le pionnier John C. Fremont conduit une expédition militaire américaine à Las Vegas pour dresser la carte du territoire.

**1854**  Monthly mail route through Las Vegas Springs established by Congress.

Der Kongress ordnet eine monatliche, durch Las Vegas Springs führende Postroute an.

Le Congrès décide la création d'une ligne postale mensuelle traversant Las Vegas.

**1855**  Mission established by colony of thirty Mormons, who depart two years later due to internal strife and Indian raid.

30 Mormonen gründen Missionsstation, die sie aber zwei Jahre später wegen interner Streitigkeiten und einem Indianerüberfall wieder aufgeben.

Une colonie d'une trentaine de mormons s'y établit. Elle partira deux ans plus tard suite à des querelles internes et à un raid indien.

**1862**  Union Pacific Railroad granted charter by Congress to construct portion of transcontinental railroad connecting with Central Pacific Railroad at California-Nevada border. Small outpost develops at Las Vegas Springs.

Union Pacific Railroad erhält vom Kongress die Konzession, den Abschnitt der transkontinentalen Eisenbahn zu bauen, der bis zum Zusammenschluss mit der Central Pacific Railroad an der Grenze von Kalifornien und Nevada noch fehlt. Kleine Niederlassung in Las Vegas Springs.

L'Union Pacific Railroad est chargée par le Congrès de construire un tronçon de la ligne de chemin de fer transcontinentale rejoignant la Central Pacific Railroad à la frontière de la Californie et du Nevada. Établissement de petits postes avancés aux « Sources de Vegas ».

**1905**  Land-auction for sale of Las Vegas conducted by railroad. Official town-site of Las Vegas is born. Completion of rail route between Salt Lake City and Los Angeles. Hotel Las Vegas, the town's first hotel, is built.

Die Eisenbahn versteigert Las Vegas. Offizielle Stadtgründung. Fertigstellung der Bahnstrecke zwischen Salt Lake City und Los Angeles. Das erste Hotel der Stadt, Hotel Las Vegas, wird gebaut.

Vente aux enchères de terrains à Las Vegas organisée par les chemins de fer. Naissance officielle de la ville de Las Vegas. Achèvement de la liaison ferroviaire entre Salt Lake City et Los Angeles. Construction de l'Hotel Las Vegas, le premier de la ville.

**1906**  Sale of liquor confined to red-light district known as Block 16.

Der Alkoholausschank wird auf den Rotlichtbezirk beschränkt, der als „Block 16" bekannt ist.

La vente d'alcool est limitée au quartier chaud, connu sous le nom de « Block 16 ».

**1910**  At midnight on 1 October, all forms of gambling prohibited.

Ab Mitternacht des 1. Oktober sind alle Formen des Glücksspiels verboten.

Le 1er octobre à minuit, toutes les formes de jeux sont interdites.

**1914** Construction begins on Los Angeles Highway (Route 91).

Baubeginn des Los Angeles Highway (Route 91).

Début de la construction de la Los Angeles Highway (Route 91).

**1931** Construction begins on Hoover Dam and Lake Mead, at cost of nearly $49 million. Gambling legalized. Residency requirement for divorce cut from three months to six weeks. Town's first luxury nightclub-casino-hotel, the Meadows, opens on Boulder Highway.

Die Bauarbeiten am Hoover-Staudamm und Stausee Lake Mead beginnen, Gesamtkosten: fast 49 Millionen US-Dollar. Das Glücksspiel wird wieder erlaubt. Die erforderliche Dauer des Wohnsitzes für Ehescheidung wird auf sechs Wochen verkürzt. Das erste Luxushotel mit Nachtclub und Spielkasino, das Meadows, eröffnet am Boulder Highway.

Démarrage de la construction du barrage Hoover et du lac Mead, coûtant selon le chiffre prévisionnel 49 millions de dollars. Le jeu est légalisé. La durée légale de résidence pour obtenir le divorce passe de trois mois à six semaines. Le premier hôtel-nightclub-casino de luxe de la ville, le Meadows, ouvre sur la Boulder Highway.

**1932** Town's first hundred-room, three-story hotel, the Apache, opens.

Das erste Hotel im Ort mit drei Stockwerken und über 100 Zimmern, das Apache, eröffnet.

Ouverture de l'Apache, premier hôtel d'une centaine de chambres, et de trois étages, de la ville.

**1934** The first neon lights up Las Vegas at Boulder Club outside of town.

Der außerhalb gelegene Boulder Club bringt die erste Neonreklame in Las Vegas an.

Apparition des premiers néons au Boulder Club, situé en dehors de la ville.

**1935** Hoover Dam unveiled by President Franklin D. Roosevelt.

Der Hoover-Staudamm wird von Präsident Franklin D. Roosevelt eingeweiht.

Le barrage Hoover est inauguré par le Président Franklin D. Roosevelt.

**1938** Gambling and prostitution crackdown in Hollywood.

In Hollywood wird das Verbot von Glücksspiel und Prostitution durchgesetzt.

Hollywood part en guerre contre le jeu et la prostitution.

**1941** Las Vegas leases property for development of new military airfield to US Army. Prostitution banned. First resort, El Rancho Vegas, opens on what will become "the Strip".

Las Vegas verpachtet Land für einen neuen Luftwaffenstützpunkt an die US Army. Prostitution wird verboten. Am später so genannten „Strip" eröffnet das erste Resort-hotel, das El Rancho Vegas.

Las Vegas signe un contrat de bail avec l'armée américaine pour la construction d'un nouveau terrain d'aviation militaire. La prostitution est interdite. Ouverture du premier complexe hôtelier, El Rancho Vegas, sur ce qui va devenir le Strip.

**1942** Fifteen miles southeast, Basic Magnesium plant opens to support war effort. Town of Henderson created to handle influx of thousands of workers. Last Frontier resort opens on the Strip.

25 Kilometer südöstlich von Las Vegas nimmt die Basic-Magnesium-Fabrik die Produktion von kriegswichtigen Materialien auf. Die Stadt Henderson entsteht, die Tausenden Arbeitern Wohnraum bietet. Das Resorthotel Last Frontier eröffnet am Strip.

A vingt-cinq kilomètres au sud-est s'ouvre une usine de production de magnésium pour soutenir l'effort de guerre. Création de la ville de Henderson pour absorber le flot d'ouvriers. Ouverture du Last Frontier sur le Strip.

**1944** Sophie Tucker first world-famous star to perform in Las Vegas. Twenty-five-year-old Vegas mainstay Liberace makes his debut at Last Frontier. Gambling revenues jump 56 percent from 1941.

Sophie Tucker ist der erste Weltstar, der in Las Vegas auftritt. Der legendäre Entertainer Liberace, der Vegas bis ans Lebensende treu bleibt, gibt sein Debüt im Last Fron-

tier. Einnahmen aus dem Glücksspiel sind 56 Prozent höher als 1941.

Sophie Tucker est la première star internationale à se produire à Las Vegas. Le jeune Liberace, vingt-cinq ans et futur pilier de Las Vegas, fait ses débuts au Last Frontier. Les revenus du jeu augmentent de cinquante-six pour cent en 1941.

**1946** Flamingo Hotel opens as first "super resort" on the Strip, ushering in modern Las Vegas. Jimmy Durante headlines.

Das Flamingo Hotel eröffnet als erstes „Superresort" am Strip und wird Vorbote des modernen Las Vegas. Auftritte von Jimmy Durante.

Ouverture du Flamingo Hotel, annoncé comme le premier « super hôtel », et qui ouvre la voie au Las Vegas moderne. Jimmy Durante est à l'affiche.

**1947** Lena Horne performs at Flamingo. Bill "Bojangles" Robinson plays Flamingo billed as "The World's Greatest Dancer". Black performers still barred from eating or sleeping at hotels.

Lena Horne tritt im Flamingo auf. Bill „Bojangles" Robinson wird im Flamingo als „der beste Tänzer der Welt" angekündigt. Schwarze Künstler dürfen in den Hotels weder essen noch übernachten.

Lena Horne chante au Flamingo. Bill Bojangles s'y produit également et on le présente comme « le plus grand danseur du monde ». Les artistes noirs n'ont toujours pas le droit de se restaurer ni de dormir dans les hôtels.

**1948** Thunderbird gambling resort opens on the Strip. Dean Martin and Jerry Lewis debut at Flamingo. McCarran Field dedicated as county airport.

Das Glücksspiel-Resorthotel Thunderbird eröffnet am Strip. Erster Auftritt von Dean Martin und Jerry Lewis im Flamingo. Der Flughafen McCarran Field wird eingeweiht.

Ouverture sur le Strip de la maison de jeux Thunderbird. Dean Martin et Jerry Lewis débutent au Flamingo. McCarran Field devient l'aéroport du Comté.

**1950** Three hundred-room Desert Inn opens on the Strip.

Das 300-Zimmer-Hotel Desert Inn eröffnet am Strip.

Le Desert Inn, un établissement de trois cent chambres, ouvre sur le Strip.

**1951** Atomic Energy Commission tests first of several atomic bombs at Nevada Test Site, northwest of city. Crooner Frank Sinatra performs in Las Vegas for the first time at Desert Inn.

Die US-Atomenergiekommission führt die ersten Atombombentest am Nevada Test Site nordwestlich der Stadt durch. Der Sänger Frank Sinatra hat seinen ersten Auftritt in Las Vegas im Desert Inn.

La commission à l'Énergie atomique effectue des essais nucléaires sur le Nevada Test Site, au nord-ouest de la ville. Frank Sinatra se produit pour la première fois à Las Vegas, au Desert Inn.

**1952** Sahara opens on the Strip with two hundred rooms, soon followed by Sands resort. Danny Thomas headlines.

Das Sahara mit 200 Gästezimmern eröffnet am Strip, gefolgt vom Sands Resort. Auf der Bühne steht Danny Thomas.

Le Sahara, deux cents chambres, ouvre sur le Strip, bientôt suivi par le Sands. Danny Thomas fait la une des journaux.

**1953** Marlene Dietrich commands $30 000 a week to perform at Sahara.

Marlene Dietrich verlangt 30 000 Dollar pro Woche für ihre Auftritte im Sahara.

Marlene Dietrich obtient 30 000 dollars de salaire hebdomadaire pour se produire au Sahara.

**1955** Royal Nevada opens on the Strip, costing $5 million. At nine stories, the Riviera is first high-rise on the Strip. The Dunes is third major resort to open.

Das 5 Millionen Dollar teure Royal Nevada wird am Strip eröffnet. Das Riviera mit seinen neun Stockwerken ist das erste Hochhaus am Strip. Das Dunes eröffnet als drittes Luxushotel.

Ouverture sur le Strip du Royal Nevada, d'un coût de 5 millions de dollars. Avec ses neuf étages, le Riviera est la première construction en hauteur du Strip. Le Dunes est le troisième grand complexe hôtelier à ouvrir ses portes.

**1956** Elvis Presley flops in first Las Vegas performance at New Frontier (formerly Last Frontier). Judy Garland has better success there. The Fremont opens downtown. At fifteen stories, it is the tallest building in Nevada.

Bei seinem ersten Auftritt in Las Vegas im New Frontier (ehemals Last Frontier) hat Elvis Presley keinen Erfolg. Judy Garland ist dort wesentlich populärer. In Downtown eröffnet das Fremont, mit 15 Stokkwerken das höchste Gebäude Nevadas.

Pour sa première apparition à Las Vegas, au New Frontier (anciennement Last Frontier), Elvis Presley fait un flop. Judy Garland y rencontre quant à elle le succès. Ouverture du Fremont dans le sud de la ville. Avec ses quinze étages, c'est la plus haute construction du Nevada.

**1957** Tropicana opens at record-breaking cost of $15 million. Singer Eddie Fisher is main attraction.

Das Tropicana, dessen Bau die Rekordsumme von 15 Millionen Dollar verschlang, eröffnet. Hauptattraktion ist der Sänger Eddie Fisher.

Ouverture du Tropicana dont le coût de construction, 15 millions de dollars, bat tous les records. Le chanteur Eddie Fisher en est la vedette.

**1958** World's largest resort, the thousand-room Stardust, opens on the Strip.

Das größte Resorthotel der Welt, das Stardust mit 1 000 Zimmern, eröffnet am Strip.

Ouverture sur le Strip du plus grand complexe hotelier au monde : le Stardust (1 000 chambres).

**1959** Gaming Control Act is passed, giving full authority to five-member commission to grant or deny gaming licenses. Las Vegas Convention Center opens on Paradise Road.

Das Glücksspielkontrollgesetz wird erlassen, wodurch eine fünfköpfige Kommission das alleinige Recht erhält, Glücksspiellizenzen zu vergeben oder zu verweigern. Das Las Vegas Convention Center an der Paradise Road wird eröffnet.

Adoption du Gaming Control Act qui donne à une commission de cinq membres le droit d'accorder ou de refuser les licences de jeu. Le Las Vegas Convention Center ouvre sur Paradise Road.

**1960** Rat Pack takes time off from filming *Ocean's Eleven* to play the Sands.

Die „Rat Pack"-Entertainer treten parallel zu den Dreharbeiten des ersten *Ocean's Eleven* im Sands auf.

Le « Rat Pack » profite de son temps libre sur le tournage de *L'inconnu de Las Vegas* pour se produire au Sands.

**1963** Diva Barbra Streisand hits the stage at Riviera as Liberace's guest.

Die Diva Barbra Streisand zeigt sich im Riviera als Liberaces Gast auf der Bühne.

Barbra Streisand fait un triomphe en tant qu'invitée de Liberace au Riviera.

**1964** Talk-show host Johnny Carson headlines at Sahara. Convention Center venue for the Beatles' only two-concert engagement in history.

Starauftritte des Talkshow-Moderators Johnny Carson im Sahara. Die Beatles spielen im Convention Center zum einzigen Mal in ihrer Geschichte zwei Konzerte nacheinander.

L'animateur Johnny Carson est à l'affiche du Sahara. Le Convention Center accueille les Beatles pour seulement deux concerts, fait unique dans l'histoire de Las Vegas.

**1965** Heavyweight champion Muhammad Ali successfully defends his crown in bout with Floyd Patterson.

Schwergewichtsweltmeister Muhammad Ali verteidigt seinen Titel erfolgreich gegen Floyd Patterson.

Le champion du monde des poids lourds Muhammad Ali défend avec succès son titre contre Floyd Patterson.

**1966** New theme resorts on the Strip, the Aladdin and Caesars Palace open. Millionaire Howard Hughes arrives in Las Vegas and begins his buying spree.

Die neuen Themenhotels Aladdin und Caesars Palace eröffnen am

Strip. Der Millionär Howard Hughes kommt nach Las Vegas und beginnt mit dem Aufkauf von Hotels.

Nouveaux complexes hôteliers à thèmes sur le Strip et ouverture de l'Aladdin et du Caesars Palace. Arrivée à Las Vegas du milliardaire Howard Hughes et début de sa série d'acquisitions.

**1967** Elvis Presley and Priscilla Beaulieu wed at the Aladdin. Corporate Gaming Act approved, allowing publicly traded companies to buy hotel-casinos.

Elvis Presley und Priscilla Beaulieu heiraten im Aladdin. Das Unternehmensglücksspielgesetz wird erlassen, mit dem Aktiengesellschaften die Erlaubnis erhalten, Kasinohotels zu kaufen.

Elvis Presley et Priscilla Beaulieu se marient à l'Aladdin. Adoption du Corporate Gaming Act qui permet à des entreprises reconnues d'acquérir des hôtels-casinos.

**1968** Family oriented hotel-casino Circus Circus opens.

Das auf Familien zugeschnittene Kasinohotel Circus Circus wird eröffnet.

Ouverture de l'hôtel-casino Circus Circus qui vise une clientèle familiale.

**1969** Landmark hotel and Las Vegas Hilton open next door to Convention Center. Elvis Presley returns to Las Vegas stage after thirteen years.

Neben dem Convention Center werden das Landmark Hotel und das Las Vegas Hilton eröffnet. 13 Jahre nach dem ersten Anlauf tritt Elvis Presley wieder in Las Vegas auf.

L'hôtel Landmark et le Las Vegas Hilton ouvrent juste à côté du Convention Center. Elvis remonte sur une scène de Las Vegas pour la première fois depuis treize ans.

**1970** Howard Hughes vacates Las Vegas and moves to Paradise Island, Nassau.

Howard Hughes verlässt Las Vegas und zieht nach Paradise Island, Nassau.

Howard Hughes quitte Las Vegas pour l'île paradisiaque de Nassau.

**1972** World's largest resort, MGM Grand, opens on the Strip with 2100 rooms. Dean Martin is star attraction.

Das größte Resorthotel der Welt, das MGM Grand mit 2100 Zimmern, wird am Strip eröffnet. Hauptattraktion ist Dean Martin.

Le plus grand complexe hôtelier du monde, le MGM Grand, d'une capacité de 2100 chambres, ouvre sur le Strip. Dean Martin en est la vedette.

**1978** 50 percent of county's increase in revenue from gaming comes from dollar slot machines. World heavyweight Leon Spinks defeats Muhammad Ali at Las Vegas Hilton.

50 Prozent der Zuwächse bei den Glücksspieleinnahmen in Las Vegas County stammen aus einarmigen Banditen mit einem Dollar Einsatz. Muhammad Ali verliert im Las Vegas Hilton seinen Weltmeistertitel an Leon Spinks.

Cinquante pour cent des revenus du jeu dans le Comté proviennent des machines à sous. Le champion du monde des poids lourds Leon Spinks bat Muhammad Ali au Las Vegas Hilton.

**1979** Caesars Palace opens the Omnimax theater and hosts a sixty-fourth birthday party for Frank Sinatra. Vegas World opens.

Das Caesars Palace weiht das Omnimax Theater ein und veranstaltet eine Party zu Ehren von Frank Sinatras 64. Geburtstag. Vegas World wird eröffnet.

Le Caesars Palace ouvre la salle Omnimax et organise une fête pour les soixante-quatre ans de Frank Sinatra. Ouverture du Vegas World.

**1980** Las Vegas celebrates its seventy-fifth birthday. Larry Holmes beats Muhammad Ali in a specially constructed $1-million stadium at Caesars Palace.

Las Vegas feiert seinen 75. Geburtstag. In einem eigens auf dem Parkplatz des Caesars Palace errichteten, eine Million Dollar teuren Stadion schlägt Larry Holmes Muhammad Ali.

Las Vegas célèbre ses soixante-quinze ans. Larry Holmes défait Muhammad Ali dans un stade

d'un million de dollars construit spécialement pour l'occasion.

**1981** Dolly Parton performs at Riviera, commanding $350 000 a week. $10-million show *Jubilee!* most expensive ever produced in Entertainment Capital. Siegfried and Roy open at Frontier.

Dolly Parton erhält für ihre Auftritte im Riviera 350 000 Dollar pro Woche. Mit zehn Millionen Dollar ist die Revue *Jubilee!* die teuerste Produktion, die es je in der Unterhaltungsmetropole gab. Siegfried und Roy eröffnen ihre Show im Frontier.

Dolly Parton se produit au Riviera pour un cachet hebdomadaire de 350 000 dollars. Avec un coût de 10 millions de dollars, *Jubilee* est le show le plus cher jamais produit dans la capitale du divertissement. Siegfried et Roy présentent leur spectacle de magie au Frontier.

**1986** With 14.2 million visitors, Las Vegas records best tourism year.

Mit 14,2 Millionen Besuchern verbucht Las Vegas das bis dahin beste Jahr für den Tourismus.

Las Vegas accueille 14,2 millions de visiteurs, un record encore invaincu à ce jour.

**1989** Steve Wynn opens Mirage on the Strip, making it the largest private hotel world-wide.

Steve Wynn eröffnet am Strip das Mirage, das größte Hotel der Welt in Privatbesitz.

Steve Wynn ouvre sur le Strip le Mirage, le plus grand hôtel du monde.

**1990** Excalibur opens.

Das Excalibur wird eröffnet.

Ouverture de l'Excalibur.

**1993** Luxor, Treasure Island and the renovated MGM Grand hotel and theme park open. Each exceeds 2 000-room mark.

Luxor, Treasure Island und das renovierte MGM Grand mit Freizeitpark öffnen ihre Türen. Jedes dieser Hotels hat mehr als 2 000 Zimmer.

Ouverture du Luxor, du Treasure Island et réouverture du grand hôtel et parc à thèmes MGM après rénovation. Chacun d'eux a plus de deux mille chambres.

**1997** New York-New York opens.

Das New York-New York wird eröffnet.

Le New York-New York ouvre ses portes.

**1998** Bellagio opens, heralding new era of super resorts.

Mit der Eröffnung des Bellagio beginnt die neue Ära der Superresorts.

Ouverture du Bellagio qui inaugure une ère nouvelle de méga-structures hôtelières.

**1999** Mandalay Bay, the Venetian and Paris Las Vegas open.

Mandalay Bay, Venetian und Paris Las Vegas werden eröffnet.

Ouverture du Mandalay Bay, du Venetian et du Paris Las Vegas.

ACKNOWLEDGEMENTS

The editor would like to thank W. R. Wilkerson III for telling the story of Vegas as only he can; Alan Hess for lending his knowledgeable eye; and Lisa Wagner Holley for providing a royal flush in designing the book. A roll of the dice goes out to Ralph Bowman, Dan De Palma, Jeff and Patty Carr, Gary Fredericks and the countless other vendors at flea markets and paper shows across the good ol' US of A for providing the Vegas images found herein.

Editor: Jim Heimann, Los Angeles
Design: Lisa Wagner Holley, Los Angeles
Digital scans: Artworks, Pasadena
Production: Tina Ciborowius, Cologne
Project management: Sonja Altmeppen, Cologne
English-language editor: Nina Wiener, Los Angeles
German translation: Anke Caroline Burger, Berlin
French translation: Patrick Javault, Strasbourg
Collaboration: Anna Peccianti and Ethel Seno, Los Angeles

© 2003 TASCHEN GmbH
Hohenzollernring 53, D-50672 Köln
www.taschen.com

Printed in Italy
ISBN 3-8228-2620-0

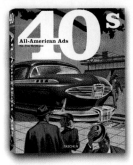

**All-American Ads of the 40s**
W.R. Wilkerson III, Ed. Jim
Heimann / Flexi-cover, 768 pp. /
€ 29.99 / $ 39.99 / £ 19.99 /
¥ 4.900

**All-American Ads of the 50s**
Ed. Jim Heimann / Flexi-cover,
928 pp. / € 29.99 / $ 39.99 /
£ 19.99 / ¥ 4.900

**All-American Ads of the 60s**
Steven Heller, Ed. Jim Heimann /
Flexi-cover, 960 pp. / € 29.99 /
$ 39.99 / £ 19.99 / ¥ 4.900

## "The ads do more than advertise products – they provide a record of American everyday life of a bygone era in a way that nothing else can." —*Associated Press*, USA

## " Buy them all and add some pleasure to your life."

**All-American Ads 40ˢ**
Ed. Jim Heimann

**All-American Ads 50ˢ**
Ed. Jim Heimann

**All-American Ads 60ˢ**
Ed. Jim Heimann

**Angels**
Gilles Néret

**Architecture Now!**
Ed. Philip Jodidio

**Art Now**
Eds. Burkhard Riemschneider,
Uta Grosenick

**Atget's Paris**
Ed. Hans Christian Adam

**Best of Bizarre**
Ed. Eric Kroll

**Bizarro Postcards**
Ed. Jim Heimann

**Karl Blossfeldt**
Ed. Hans Christian Adam

**California, Here I Come**
Ed. Jim Heimann

**50ˢ Cars**
Ed. Jim Heimann

**Chairs**
Charlotte & Peter Fiell

**Classic Rock Covers**
Michael Ochs

**Description of Egypt**
Ed. Gilles Néret

**Design of the 20ᵗʰ Century**
Charlotte & Peter Fiell

**Design for the 21ˢᵗ Century**
Charlotte & Peter Fiell

**Dessous**
Lingerie as Erotic Weapon
Gilles Néret

**Devils**
Gilles Néret

**Digital Beauties**
Ed. Julius Wiedemann

**Robert Doisneau**
Ed. Jean-Claude Gautrand

**Eccentric Style**
Ed. Angelika Taschen

**Encyclopaedia Anatomica**
Museo La Specola, Florence

**Erotica 17ᵗʰ–18ᵗʰ Century**
From Rembrandt to Fragonard
Gilles Néret

**Erotica 19ᵗʰ Century**
From Courbet to Gauguin
Gilles Néret

**Erotica 20ᵗʰ Century, Vol. I**
From Rodin to Picasso
Gilles Néret

**Erotica 20ᵗʰ Century, Vol. II**
From Dalí to Crumb
Gilles Néret

**Future Perfect**
Ed. Jim Heimann

**The Garden at Eichstätt**
Basilius Besler

**HR Giger**
HR Giger

**Homo Art**
Gilles Néret

**Hula**
Ed. Jim Heimann

**India Bazaar**
Samantha Harrison,
Bari Kumar

**Indian Style**
Ed. Angelika Taschen

**Industrial Design**
Charlotte & Peter Fiell

**Kitchen Kitsch**
Ed. Jim Heimann

**Krazy Kids' Food**
Eds. Steve Roden,
Dan Goodsell

**Las Vegas**
Ed. Jim Heimann

**London Style**
Ed. Angelika Taschen

**Male Nudes**
David Leddick

**Man Ray**
Ed. Manfred Heiting

**Mexicana**
Ed. Jim Heimann

**Native Americans**
Edward S. Curtis
Ed. Hans Christian Adam

**New York Style**
Ed. Angelika Taschen

**Extra/Ordinary Objects,
Vol. I**
Ed. Colors Magazine

**Extra/Ordinary Objects,
Vol. II**
Ed. Colors Magazine

**15ᵗʰ Century Paintings**
Rose-Marie & Rainer Hagen

**16ᵗʰ Century Paintings**
Rose-Marie & Rainer Hagen

**Paris-Hollywood**
Serge Jacques
Ed. Gilles Néret

**Penguin**
Frans Lanting

**Photo Icons, Vol. I**
Hans-Michael Koetzle

**Photo Icons, Vol. II**
Hans-Michael Koetzle

**20ᵗʰ Century Photography**
Museum Ludwig Cologne

**Pin-Ups**
Ed. Burkhard Riemschneider

**Giovanni Battista Piranesi**
Luigi Ficacci

**Provence Style**
Ed. Angelika Taschen

**Pussy Cats**
Gilles Néret

**Redouté's Roses**
Pierre-Joseph Redouté

**Robots and Spaceships**
Ed. Teruhisa Kitahara

**Seaside Style**
Ed. Angelika Taschen

**See the World**
Ed. Jim Heimann

**Eric Stanton**
Reunion in Ropes & Other
Stories
Ed. Burkhard Riemschneider

**Eric Stanton**
She Dominates All & Other
Stories
Ed. Burkhard Riemschneider

**Tattoos**
Ed. Henk Schiffmacher

**Tuscany Style**
Ed. Angelika Taschen

**Edward Weston**
Ed. Manfred Heiting

**Women Artists**
in the 20ᵗʰ and 21ˢᵗ Century
Ed. Uta Grosenick

# LAS VEGAS

*magazine*

# ATOM BOMB BLASTS

ACTUAL PICTURES
PHOTOGRAPHED FROM VANTAG[E]
POINT HIGH ATOP MOUNT
CHARLESTON, NEAR LAS VEGAS

★

ICONS